Teach Your Child to Read

300 Short Easy Sentences

English - Greek

Name 

I Can...

- read the 1st sentence.
- read the 2nd sentence.
- make a sentence from a picture.
- color a picture.
- Draw a picture.

The frog is going to a party.

Ο βάτραχος πηγαίνει σε πάρτι.

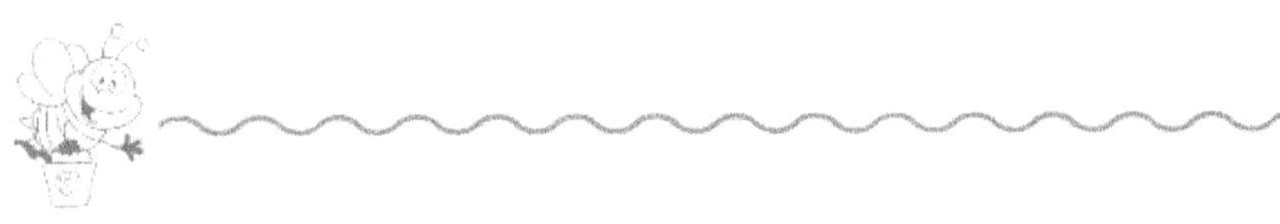

The happy frog is wearing a green hat.

Ο ευτυχισμένος βάτραχος φοράει ένα πράσινο καπέλο.

Name

I Can...

- ☐ read the 1st sentence.
- ☐ read the 2nd sentence.
- ☐ make a sentence from a picture.
- ☐ color a picture.
- ☐ Draw a picture.

Owl likes to read big books.

Η κουκουβάγια αρέσει να διαβάζει μεγάλα βιβλία.

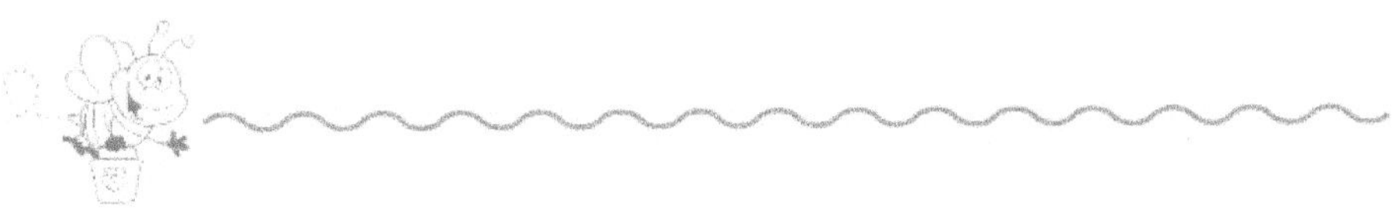

A smart owl is reading an alphabet book.

Μια έξυπνη κουκουβάγια διαβάζει ένα βιβλίο αλφάβητου.

Name 

I Can...

- [ ] read the 1st sentence.
- [ ] read the 2nd sentence.
- [ ] make a sentence from a picture.
- [ ] color a picture.
- [ ] Draw a picture.

Come on! The ice cream truck is here!

Ελα! Το παγωτό φορτηγό είναι εδώ!

He is driving a big icecream truck.

Οδηγεί ένα μεγάλο φορτηγό παγωτού.

Name _______________ 

I Can...

- [ ] read the 1st sentence.
- [ ] read the 2nd sentence.
- [ ] make a sentence from a picture.
- [ ] color a picture.
- [ ] Draw a picture.

Dragons are very friendly and have scales on their backs.

Οι δράκοι είναι πολύ φιλικοί και έχουν κλίμακες στις πλάτες τους.

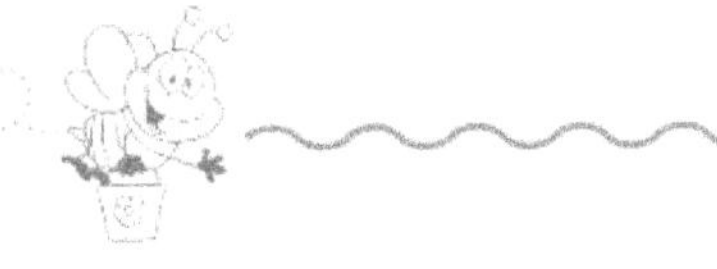 ～～～～～～～～～～～～～～～～

The dragon is waving his hand.

Ο δράκος κυματίζει το χέρι του.

Name

I Can...

- [ ] read the 1st sentence.
- [ ] read the 2nd sentence.
- [ ] make a sentence from a picture.
- [ ] color a picture.
- [ ] Draw a picture.

This ram lives in the farmhouse.

Αυτός ο κριός ζει στην αγροικία.

Ram has a large horn and fluffy wool.

Ο Ram έχει ένα μεγάλο κέρατο και αφράτο μαλλί.

Name _______________________ 

I Can...

- [ ] read the 1st sentence.
- [ ] read the 2nd sentence.
- [ ] make a sentence from a picture.
- [ ] color a picture.
- [ ] Draw a picture.

The bunny likes to eat carrots.

Το λαγουδάκι αρέσει να τρώει καρότα.

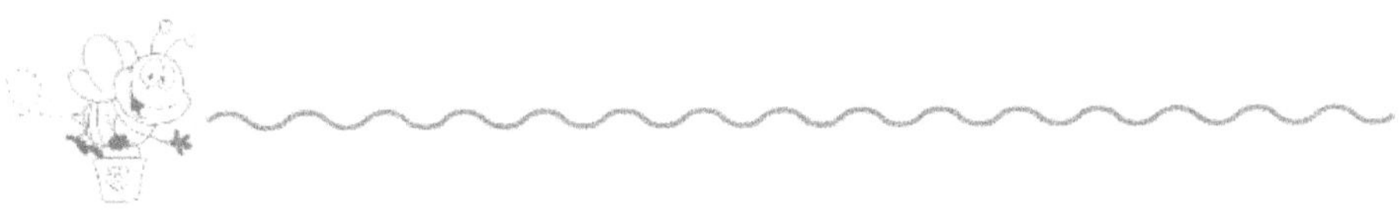

Rabbit thinks that the juicy orange carrot looks yummy.

Κουνέλι πιστεύει ότι το ζουμερό καρότο πορτοκαλιού φαίνεται yummy.

Name

I Can...

- [ ] read the 1st sentence.
- [ ] read the 2nd sentence.
- [ ] make a sentence from a picture.
- [ ] color a picture.
- [ ] Draw a picture.

The clown likes to give out balloons to little kids.

Ο κλόουν θέλει να δώσει μπαλόνια σε μικρά παιδιά.

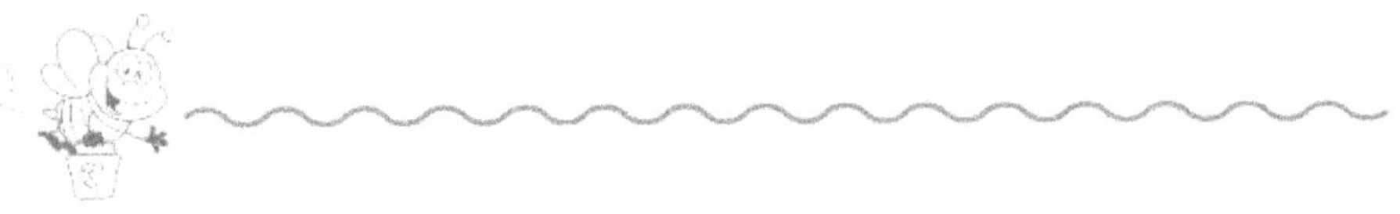

Funny, Mr. Clown is giving away colorful balloons.

Αστείος, ο κλόουν δίνει μακριά πολύχρωμα μπαλόνια.

Name

I Can...

- [ ] read the 1st sentence.
- [ ] read the 2nd sentence.
- [ ] make a sentence from a picture.
- [ ] color a picture.
- [ ] Draw a picture.

The clown is juggling balls for his performance.

Ο κλόουν ζυγίζει μπάλες για την απόδοσή του.

Talented, Mr. Clown is juggling five red balls.

Ταλαντούχος, ο κλόουν τραγουδάει πέντε κόκκινες μπάλες.

Name

I Can...

- [ ] read the 1st sentence.
- [ ] read the 2nd sentence.
- [ ] make a sentence from a picture.
- [ ] color a picture.
- [ ] Draw a picture.

The Easter Bunny is going to give out chocolate eggs.

Το Πάσχα Μπάνι πρόκειται να δώσει τα αυγά σοκολάτας.

The rabbit goes out to buy more orange carrots.

Το κουνέλι βγαίνει για να αγοράσει περισσότερα πορτοκαλιά καρότα.

Name

I Can...

- [ ] read the 1st sentence.
- [ ] read the 2nd sentence.
- [ ] make a sentence from a picture.
- [ ] color a picture.
- [ ] Draw a picture.

The pencil is drawing a zig-zag line.

Το μολύβι σχεδιάζει μια γραμμή ζιγκ-ζαγκ.

The Pencil is saying hello to you.

Το μολύβι λέει γεια σας.

Name

The pencil put on a big smile and went to work.

Το μολύβι έβαλε ένα μεγάλο χαμόγελο και πήγε στη δουλειά.

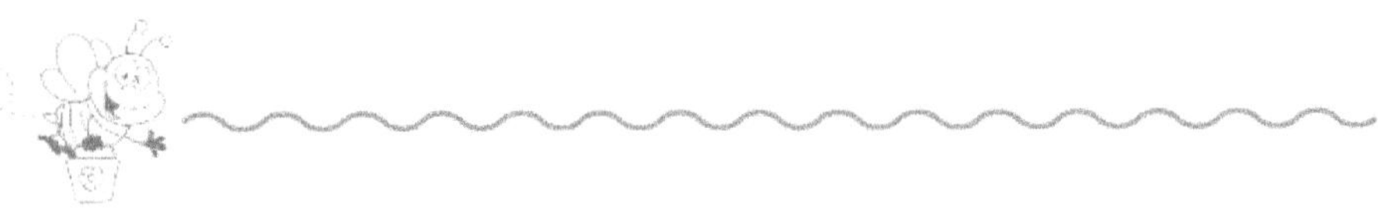

The Pencil is leaving to go on a long relaxing vacation.

Το μολύβι αφήνει να διανύσει μακρά χαλαρωτικές διακοπές.

Name ___________________ 

I Can...

- [ ] read the 1st sentence.
- [ ] read the 2nd sentence.
- [ ] make a sentence from a picture.
- [ ] color a picture.
- [ ] Draw a picture.

This snowman is my friend, and he is a helper of Santa.

Αυτός ο χιονάνθρωπος είναι ο φίλος μου και είναι βοηθός του Σάντα.

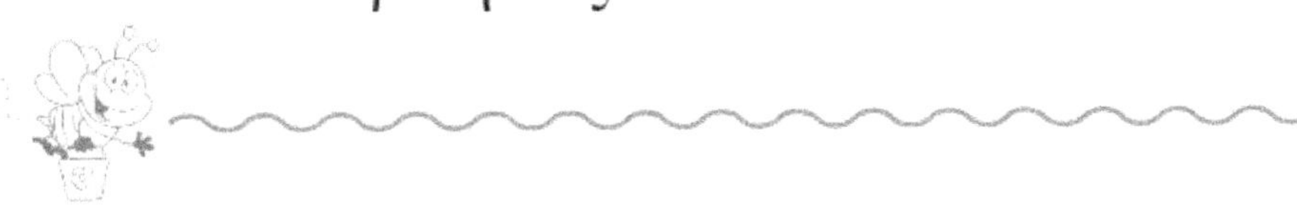

Mr. Snowman is celebrating Christmas by the decorated tree.

Ο κ. Snowman γιορτάζει τα Χριστούγεννα από το διακοσμημένο δέντρο.

I Can...

- [ ] read the 1st sentence.
- [ ] read the 2nd sentence.
- [ ] make a sentence from a picture.
- [ ] color a picture.
- [ ] Draw a picture.

The octopus is working as a chef and serving food.

Το χταπόδι δουλεύει ως σεφ και σερβίρει φαγητό.

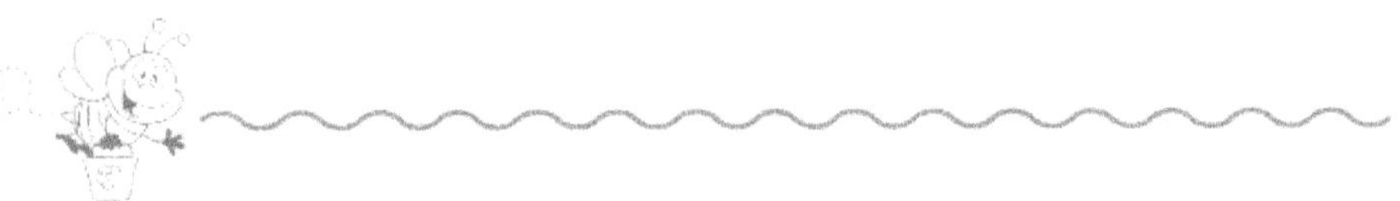

Chef Octopus is serving a delicious turkey dinner.

Ο Σεφ Χταπόδι σερβίρει ένα νόστιμο γεύμα γαλοπούλας.

I Can...

- ☐ read the 1st sentence.
- ☐ read the 2nd sentence.
- ☐ make a sentence from a picture.
- ☐ color a picture.
- ☐ Draw a picture.

Santa is happy.

Ο Σάντα είναι χαρούμενος.

Santa Claus is giving extraordinary presents to excited kids.

Ο Άγιος Βασίλης δίνει εξαιρετικά δώρα στα ενθουσιασμένα παιδιά.

Name

I Can...

- [ ] read the 1st sentence.
- [ ] read the 2nd sentence.
- [ ] make a sentence from a picture.
- [ ] color a picture.
- [ ] Draw a picture.

The bear likes to eat sweets.

Η αρκούδα αρέσει να τρώει γλυκά.

Teddy is licking a red and white candy cane.

Ο Teddy γλείφει ένα κόκκινο και λευκό ζαχαροκάλαμο.

Name

I Can...

- ☐ read the 1st sentence.
- ☐ read the 2nd sentence.
- ☐ make a sentence from a picture.
- ☐ color a picture.
- ☐ Draw a picture.

The book has a wand.

Το βιβλίο έχει μια ραβδί.

The cereal box got a magician set for Christmas.

Το κιβώτιο των δημητριακών πήρε ένα μάγο για τα Χριστούγεννα.

Name

I Can...

- [ ] read the 1st sentence.
- [ ] read the 2nd sentence.
- [ ] make a sentence from a picture.
- [ ] color a picture.
- [ ] Draw a picture.

The bear has a present.

Η αρκούδα έχει ένα δώρο.

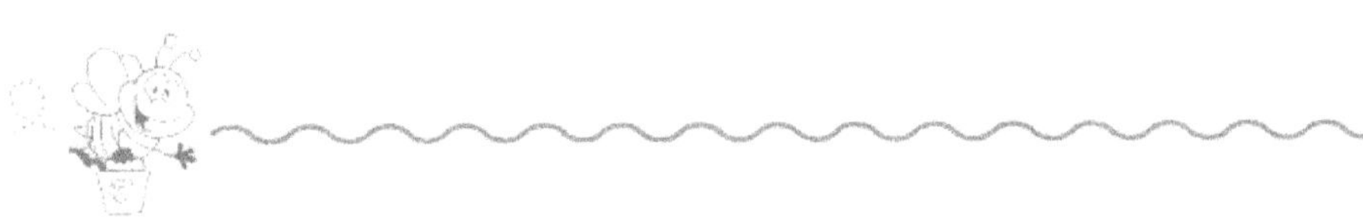

Happy Teddy is opening his box of presents from Santa.

Ο Happy Teddy ανοίγει το κουτί του από το Σάντα.

Name

I Can...

- [ ] read the 1st sentence.
- [ ] read the 2nd sentence.
- [ ] make a sentence from a picture.
- [ ] color a picture.
- [ ] Draw a picture.

Santa is going to give out presents.

Ο Σάντα πρόκειται να δώσει δώρα.

Santa is lugging a large brown bag of gifts to his sley.

Ο Σάντα αγκαλιάζει μια μεγάλη καφέ τσάντα με δώρα στο σέλεϊ του.

Name

I Can...

- [ ] read the 1st sentence.
- [ ] read the 2nd sentence.
- [ ] make a sentence from a picture.
- [ ] color a picture.
- [ ] Draw a picture.

I made a snowman.

Έκανα έναν χιονάνθρωπο.

Mr. Snowman is holding a broom and saying goodbye.

Ο κ. Χιονάνθρωπος κρατά μια σκούπα και λέει αντίο.

Name

I Can...

- [ ] read the 1st sentence.
- [ ] read the 2nd sentence.
- [ ] make a sentence from a picture.
- [ ] color a picture.
- [ ] Draw a picture.

The parrot is colorful.

Ο παπαγάλος είναι πολύχρωμος.

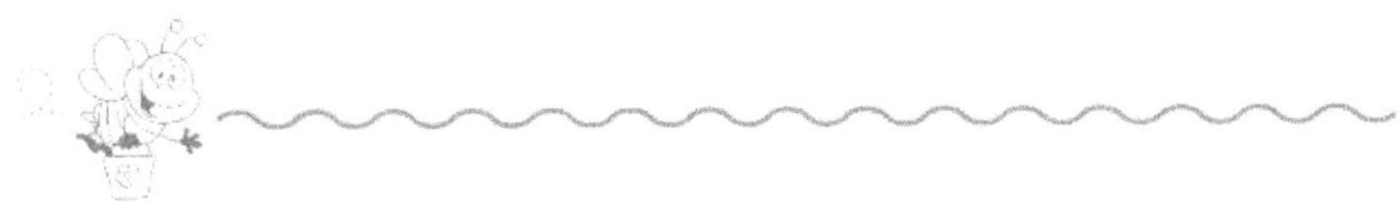

The green parrot came from the forest to the zoo.

Ο πράσινος παπαγάλος προήλθε από το δάσος στο ζωολογικό κήπο.

Name

I Can...

- [ ] read the 1st sentence.
- [ ] read the 2nd sentence.
- [ ] make a sentence from a picture.
- [ ] color a picture.
- [ ] Draw a picture.

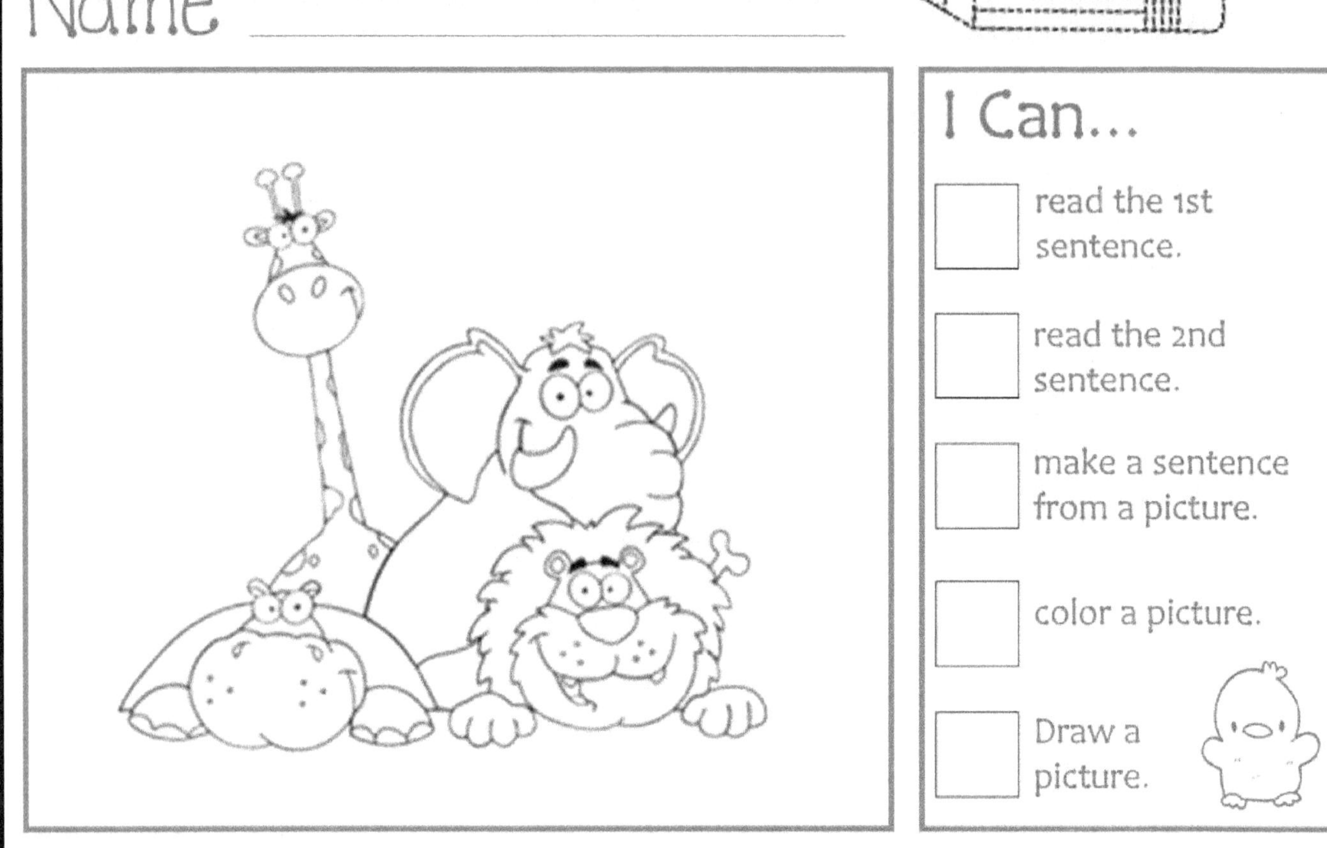

There are a lot of animals.

Υπάρχουν πολλά ζώα.

The animals are happy being together again.

Τα ζώα είναι ευτυχισμένα ξανά μαζί.

Name

I Can...

- ☐ read the 1st sentence.
- ☐ read the 2nd sentence.
- ☐ make a sentence from a picture.
- ☐ color a picture.
- ☐ Draw a picture.

The man is wearing a belt.

Ο άντρας φοράει ζώνη.

The carpenter is fixing something.

Ο ξυλουργός καθορίζει κάτι.

Name

I Can...

- [ ] read the 1st sentence.
- [ ] read the 2nd sentence.
- [ ] make a sentence from a picture.
- [ ] color a picture.
- [ ] Draw a picture.

The rabbit is very young.

Το κουνέλι είναι πολύ μικρό.

The magician plays a trick.

Ο μάγος παίζει ένα τέχνασμα.

Name

I Can...

- [ ] read the 1st sentence.
- [ ] read the 2nd sentence.
- [ ] make a sentence from a picture.
- [ ] color a picture.
- [ ] Draw a picture.

He has a potion.

Έχει ένα φίλτρο.

The scientist is making a potion.

Ο επιστήμονας κάνει ένα φίλτρο.

Name

I Can...

- [ ] read the 1st sentence.
- [ ] read the 2nd sentence.
- [ ] make a sentence from a picture.
- [ ] color a picture.
- [ ] Draw a picture.

He is wearing sunglasses.

Φοράει γυαλιά ηλίου.

The policeman is mad.

Ο αστυνομικός είναι τρελός.

Name

I Can...

- [ ] read the 1st sentence.
- [ ] read the 2nd sentence.
- [ ] make a sentence from a picture.
- [ ] color a picture.
- [ ] Draw a picture.

He has a bucket of paint.

Έχει ένα κουβά με χρώμα.

He likes to paint.

Του αρέσει να ζωγραφίζει.

Name

I Can...

- [ ] read the 1st sentence.
- [ ] read the 2nd sentence.
- [ ] make a sentence from a picture.
- [ ] color a picture.
- [ ] Draw a picture.

The man has a hat.

Ο άνθρωπος έχει ένα καπέλο.

The postman is giving out the mail in the early morning.

Ο ταχυδρόμος δίνει το ταχυδρομείο νωρίς το πρωί.

Name

I Can...

- [ ] read the 1st sentence.
- [ ] read the 2nd sentence.
- [ ] make a sentence from a picture.
- [ ] color a picture.
- [ ] Draw a picture.

He has a walkie talkie.

Έχει ένα φορητό ραδιοτηλέφωνο.

He is going to work with his suitcase.

Θα δουλέψει με τη βαλίτσα του.

Name

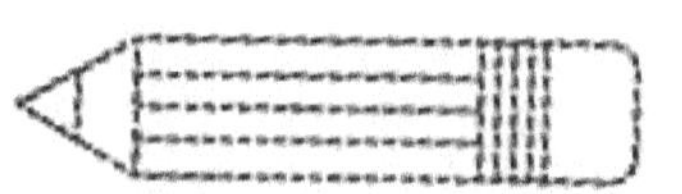

I Can...

- [ ] read the 1st sentence.
- [ ] read the 2nd sentence.
- [ ] make a sentence from a picture.
- [ ] color a picture.
- [ ] Draw a picture.

He is sleepy.

Είναι υπνηλία.

The delivery man sent us a package.

Ο άνθρωπος παράδοσης μας έστειλε ένα πακέτο.

Name

I Can...

- [ ] read the 1st sentence.
- [ ] read the 2nd sentence.
- [ ] make a sentence from a picture.
- [ ] color a picture.
- [ ] Draw a picture.

He is wearing a bowtie.

Φοράει παπιγιόν.

The waiter is serving juice.

Ο σερβιτόρος σερβίρει χυμό.

Name _______________

I Can...

- [ ] read the 1st sentence.
- [ ] read the 2nd sentence.
- [ ] make a sentence from a picture.
- [ ] color a picture.
- [ ] Draw a picture.

He has a suitcase.

Έχει μια βαλίτσα.

The engineer is holding a wrench.

Ο μηχανικός κρατάει ένα κλειδί.

Name

I Can...

- [ ] read the 1st sentence.
- [ ] read the 2nd sentence.
- [ ] make a sentence from a picture.
- [ ] color a picture.
- [ ] Draw a picture.

The chef has a napkin.

Ο σεφ έχει μια πετσέτα.

The chef serves delicious-looking food.

Ο σεφ σερβίρει νόστιμο φαγητό.

Name ____________________

I Can...

- [ ] read the 1st sentence.
- [ ] read the 2nd sentence.
- [ ] make a sentence from a picture.
- [ ] color a picture.
- [ ] Draw a picture.

The rooster has a big beak.

Ο κόκορας έχει ένα μεγάλο ράμφος.

The chicken is saying hello to us.

Το κοτόπουλο λέει γεια σε μας.

Name

I Can...

- [ ] read the 1st sentence.
- [ ] read the 2nd sentence.
- [ ] make a sentence from a picture.
- [ ] color a picture.
- [ ] Draw a picture.

The bird is small.

Το πουλί είναι μικρό.

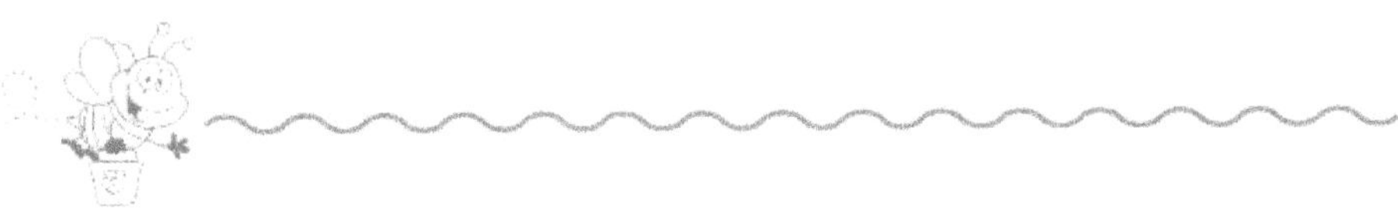

The chick is on the telephone talking with his friend.

Η γκόμενα είναι στο τηλέφωνο να μιλάει με τον φίλο του.

Name

I Can...

- [ ] read the 1st sentence.
- [ ] read the 2nd sentence.
- [ ] make a sentence from a picture.
- [ ] color a picture.
- [ ] Draw a picture.

That is my ring.

Αυτό είναι το δαχτυλίδι μου.

That is a beautiful ring.

Αυτό είναι ένα όμορφο δαχτυλίδι.

Name

I Can...

- [ ] read the 1st sentence.
- [ ] read the 2nd sentence.
- [ ] make a sentence from a picture.
- [ ] color a picture.
- [ ] Draw a picture.

The duck has three eggs.

Η πάπια έχει τρία αυγά.

The duck has a big nose.

Η πάπια έχει μια μεγάλη μύτη.

Name

I Can...

- [ ] read the 1st sentence.
- [ ] read the 2nd sentence.
- [ ] make a sentence from a picture.
- [ ] color a picture.
- [ ] Draw a picture.

The swan is beautiful.

Ο κύκνος είναι όμορφος.

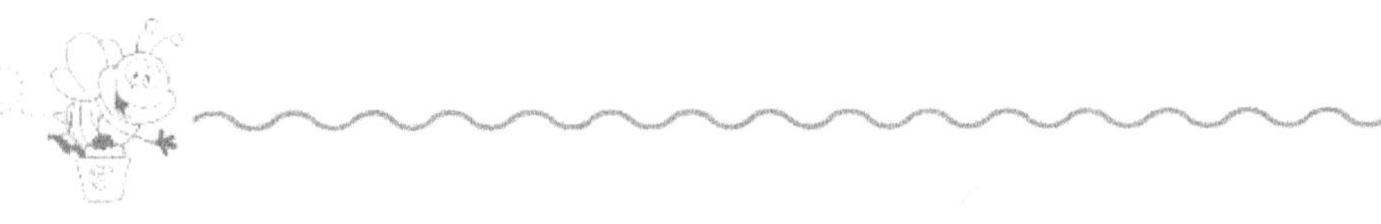

The graceful swan is striding through the water.

Ο χαριτωμένος κύκνος περνάει μέσα από το νερό.

Name

I Can...

- [ ] read the 1st sentence.
- [ ] read the 2nd sentence.
- [ ] make a sentence from a picture.
- [ ] color a picture.
- [ ] Draw a picture.

The girl is wearing a dress.

Το κορίτσι φοράει φόρεμα.

The maid is cleaning our room.

Η καμαριέρα καθαρίζει το δωμάτιό μας.

Name

I Can...

- [ ] read the 1st sentence.
- [ ] read the 2nd sentence.
- [ ] make a sentence from a picture.
- [ ] color a picture.
- [ ] Draw a picture.

The boy is running.

Το αγόρι τρέχει.

____

The little boy was running.

Το μικρό αγόρι έτρεχε.

Name

I Can...

- [ ] read the 1st sentence.
- [ ] read the 2nd sentence.
- [ ] make a sentence from a picture.
- [ ] color a picture.
- [ ] Draw a picture.

He is a musician.

Είναι μουσικός.

He is playing a lively tune on his flute.

Παίζει ζωντανή μουσική στο φλάουτο του.

I Can...

- [ ] read the 1st sentence.
- [ ] read the 2nd sentence.
- [ ] make a sentence from a picture.
- [ ] color a picture.
- [ ] Draw a picture.

He looks joyful.

Φαίνεται χαρούμενος.

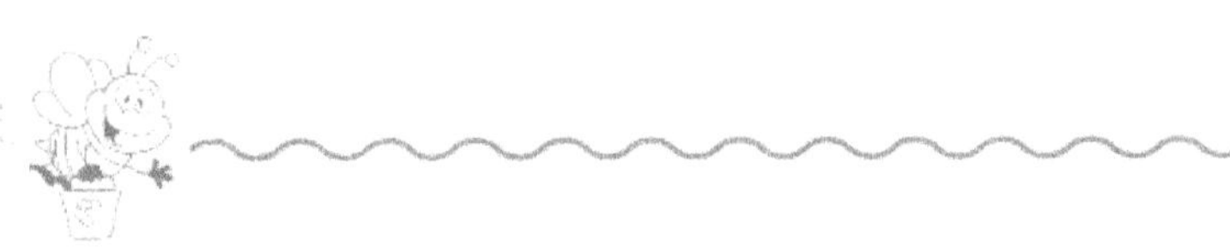

That boy works in a band and plays the drum.

Αυτό το αγόρι εργάζεται σε μια μπάντα και παίζει το τύμπανο.

Name

I Can...

- [ ] read the 1st sentence.
- [ ] read the 2nd sentence.
- [ ] make a sentence from a picture.
- [ ] color a picture.
- [ ] Draw a picture.

The dinosaur is a rock star.

Ο δεινόσαυρος είναι ένα ροκ σταρ.

The dragon is playing the guitar.

Ο δράκος παίζει κιθάρα.

Name

I Can...

- [ ] read the 1st sentence.
- [ ] read the 2nd sentence.
- [ ] make a sentence from a picture.
- [ ] color a picture.
- [ ] Draw a picture.

The nurse helps the doctor.

Η νοσοκόμα βοηθά τον γιατρό.

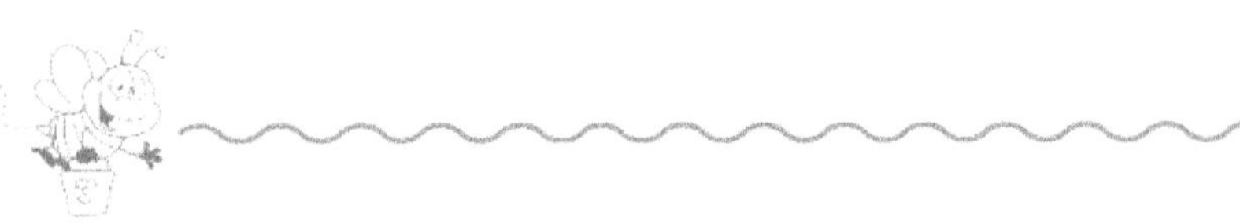

The nurse looks scary, holding a syringe.

Η νοσοκόμα φαίνεται τρομακτικό, κρατώντας μια σύριγγα.

Name

I Can...

- [ ] read the 1st sentence.
- [ ] read the 2nd sentence.
- [ ] make a sentence from a picture.
- [ ] color a picture.
- [ ] Draw a picture.

She is wearing a crown.

Φοράει στέμμα.

The queen bee has a beautiful wand.

Η βασίλισσα μέλισσα έχει μια όμορφη ραβδί.

Name

I Can...

- ☐ read the 1st sentence.
- ☐ read the 2nd sentence.
- ☐ make a sentence from a picture.
- ☐ color a picture.
- ☐ Draw a picture.

It is orange and black.

Είναι πορτοκαλί και μαύρο.

The tiger is wearing a bow on its neck.

Η τίγρη φορούσε τόξο στο λαιμό της.

Name

I Can...

- [ ] read the 1st sentence.
- [ ] read the 2nd sentence.
- [ ] make a sentence from a picture.
- [ ] color a picture.
- [ ] Draw a picture.

The boy is carrying a lot of books.

Το αγόρι μεταφέρει πολλά βιβλία.

The boy is carrying so many books!

Το αγόρι φέρνει τόσα πολλά βιβλία!

Name

I Can...

- [ ] read the 1st sentence.
- [ ] read the 2nd sentence.
- [ ] make a sentence from a picture.
- [ ] color a picture.
- [ ] Draw a picture.

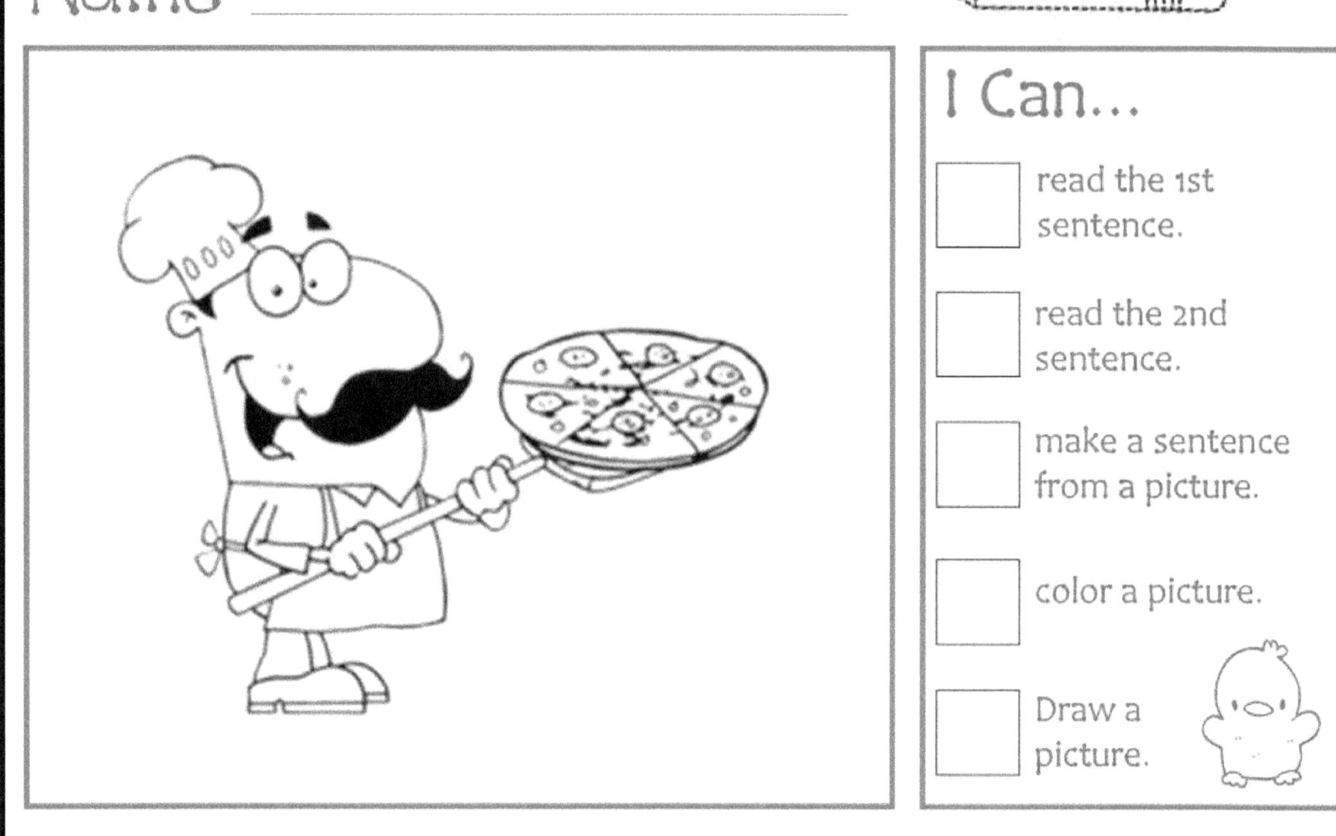

The pizza looks delicious.

Η πίτσα φαίνεται υπέροχη.

The waiter is serving steaming hot pizza.

Ο σερβιτόρος σερβίρει ατμό ζεστό πίτσα.

Name

I Can...

- [ ] read the 1st sentence.
- [ ] read the 2nd sentence.
- [ ] make a sentence from a picture.
- [ ] color a picture.
- [ ] Draw a picture.

That is my dad's computer.

Αυτός είναι ο υπολογιστής του μπαμπά μου.

My dad works on the computer.

Ο μπαμπάς μου εργάζεται στον υπολογιστή.

Name

I Can...

- [ ] read the 1st sentence.
- [ ] read the 2nd sentence.
- [ ] make a sentence from a picture.
- [ ] color a picture.
- [ ] Draw a picture.

The farmer has a beard.

Ο αγρότης έχει γενειάδα.

The gardener is going to plant flowers

Ο κηπουρός πρόκειται να φυτέψει λουλούδια

Name

I Can...

- ☐ read the 1st sentence.
- ☐ read the 2nd sentence.
- ☐ make a sentence from a picture.
- ☐ color a picture.
- ☐ Draw a picture.

The strawberry is red.

Η φράουλα είναι κόκκινη.

I love to drink strawberry juice.

Μου αρέσει να πίνω χυμό φράουλας.

Name

I Can...

- [ ] read the 1st sentence.
- [ ] read the 2nd sentence.
- [ ] make a sentence from a picture.
- [ ] color a picture.
- [ ] Draw a picture.

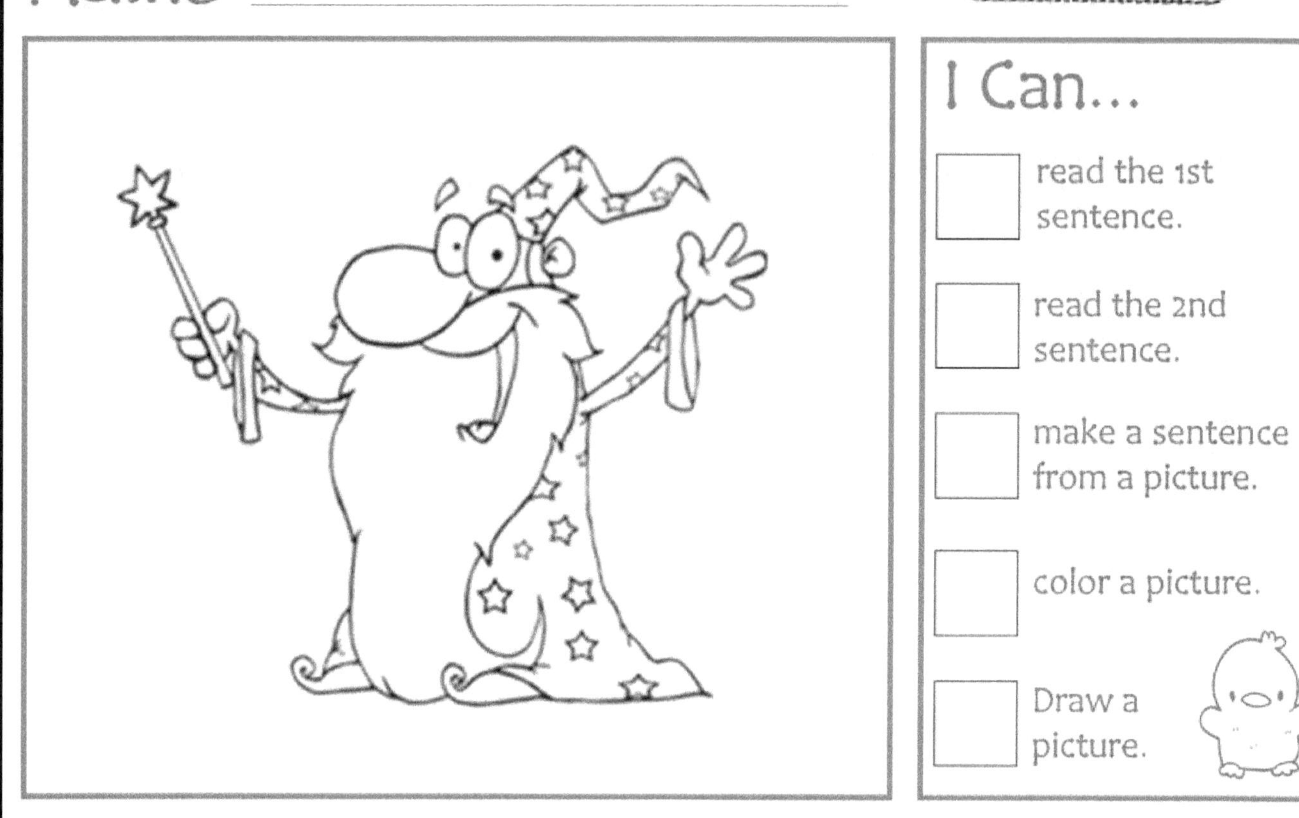

The magician has a wand.

Ο μάγος έχει μια ραβδί.

The wizard likes to work with magic.

Ο οδηγός αρέσει να δουλεύει με μαγεία.

Name _______________

I Can...

- [ ] read the 1st sentence.
- [ ] read the 2nd sentence.
- [ ] make a sentence from a picture.
- [ ] color a picture.
- [ ] Draw a picture.

Reindeer has a scarf.

Ο τάρανδος έχει κασκόλ.

Santa gave reindeer a big present.

Ο Σάντα έδωσε ταράνδου ένα μεγάλο δώρο.

Name

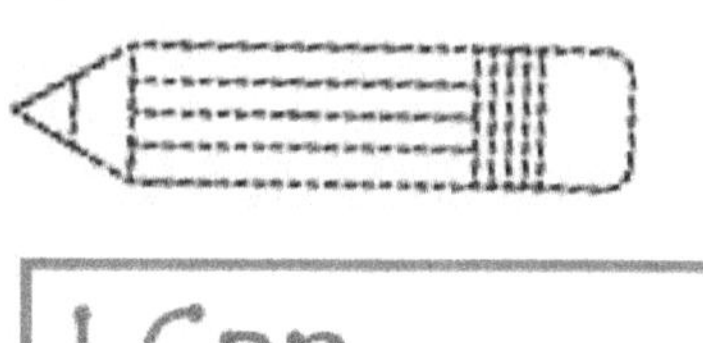

I Can...

- [ ] read the 1st sentence.
- [ ] read the 2nd sentence.
- [ ] make a sentence from a picture.
- [ ] color a picture.
- [ ] Draw a picture.

I have a lot of pencils.

Έχω πολλά μολύβια.

I have a lot of brushes and pencils.

Έχω πολλά πινέλα και μολύβια.

Name

I Can...

- [ ] read the 1st sentence.
- [ ] read the 2nd sentence.
- [ ] make a sentence from a picture.
- [ ] color a picture.
- [ ] Draw a picture.

Santa is fat.

Ο Σάντα είναι παχύς.

Santa is having fun.

Ο Σάντα διασκεδάζει.

Name 

I have one nose.

Έχω μύτη.

The one is saying its name.

Το ένα λέει το όνομά του.

Name

I Can...

- [ ] read the 1st sentence.
- [ ] read the 2nd sentence.
- [ ] make a sentence from a picture.
- [ ] color a picture.
- [ ] Draw a picture.

I have two ears.

Έχω δύο αυτιά.

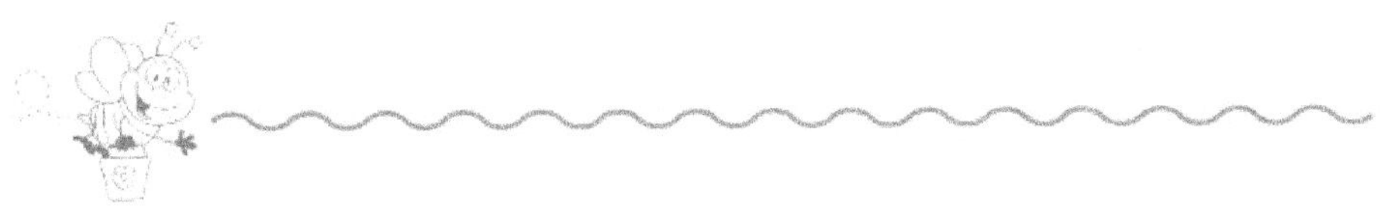

The number "two" is holding up bunny ears.

Ο αριθμός "δύο" κρατά τα αυτιά του λαγουδάκι.

Name

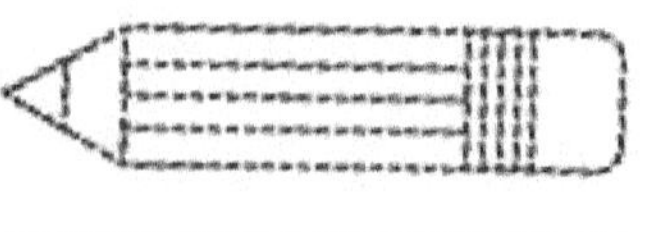

I Can...

- [ ] read the 1st sentence.
- [ ] read the 2nd sentence.
- [ ] make a sentence from a picture.
- [ ] color a picture.
- [ ] Draw a picture.

I have three buttons on my dress.

Έχω τρία κουμπιά στο φόρεμά μου.

The number "three" is saying you got 3 out of 3.

Ο αριθμός "τρεις" λέει ότι πήρατε 3 από τα 3.

Name _______________________

I Can...

- [ ] read the 1st sentence.
- [ ] read the 2nd sentence.
- [ ] make a sentence from a picture.
- [ ] color a picture.
- [ ] Draw a picture.

I have 0 tails.

Έχω 0 ουρές.

The number "zero" is saying, Ok.

Ο αριθμός "μηδέν" λέει, Εντάξει.

Name _______________

I Can...

- ☐ read the 1st sentence.
- ☐ read the 2nd sentence.
- ☐ make a sentence from a picture.
- ☐ color a picture.
- ☐ Draw a picture.

I have five fingers on 1 of my hands.

Έχω πέντε δάχτυλα σε 1 από τα χέρια μου.

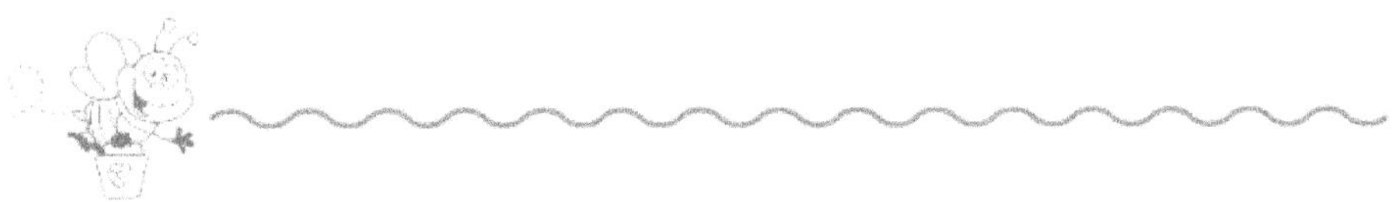

The number "five" is trying to give you a high five.

Ο αριθμός "πέντε" προσπαθεί να σας δώσει ένα υψηλό πέντε.

Name

I Can...

- [ ] read the 1st sentence.
- [ ] read the 2nd sentence.
- [ ] make a sentence from a picture.
- [ ] color a picture.
- [ ] Draw a picture.

My cat has four legs.

Η γάτα μου έχει τέσσερα πόδια.

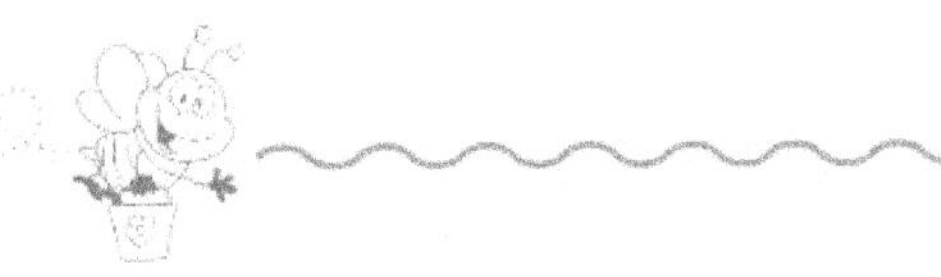

The number "four" is counting to four.

Ο αριθμός "τέσσερα" μετράει σε τέσσερα.

Name

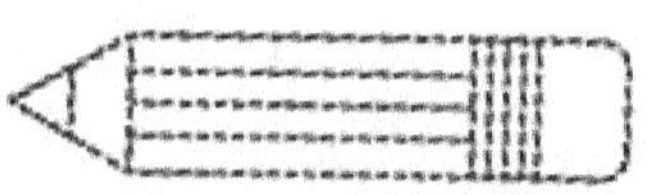

I Can...

- [ ] read the 1st sentence.
- [ ] read the 2nd sentence.
- [ ] make a sentence from a picture.
- [ ] color a picture.
- [ ] Draw a picture.

A butterfly has six legs.

Μια πεταλούδα έχει έξι πόδια.

The number "six" is saying 1+5=6.

Ο αριθμός "έξι" λέει 1 + 5 = 6.

Name

I Can...

- [ ] read the 1st sentence.
- [ ] read the 2nd sentence.
- [ ] make a sentence from a picture.
- [ ] color a picture.
- [ ] Draw a picture.

A spider has eight legs.

Μια αράχνη έχει οκτώ πόδια.

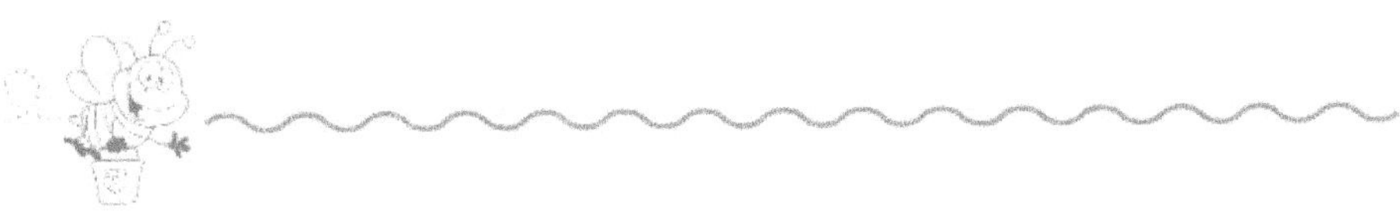

The happy and excited eight is holding up eight fingers

Το χαρούμενο και ενθουσιασμένο οκτώ κρατάει οκτώ δάχτυλα

Name

I Can...

- [ ] read the 1st sentence.
- [ ] read the 2nd sentence.
- [ ] make a sentence from a picture.
- [ ] color a picture.
- [ ] Draw a picture.

The rooster is going to wake people up.

Ο κόκορας θα ξυπνήσει τους ανθρώπους.

The rooster is on the fence.

Ο κόκορας βρίσκεται στο φράκτη.

Name

I Can...

- [ ] read the 1st sentence.
- [ ] read the 2nd sentence.
- [ ] make a sentence from a picture.
- [ ] color a picture.
- [ ] Draw a picture.

My sister has nine stuffed animals.

Η αδελφή μου έχει εννέα γεμιστά ζώα.

The smiling number nine is saying its name out loud.

Το χαμογελαστό νούμερο εννέα λέει δυνατά το όνομά του.

65

The baby bee has yellow and black stripes.

Η μέλισσα του μωρού έχει κίτρινες και μαύρες ρίγες.

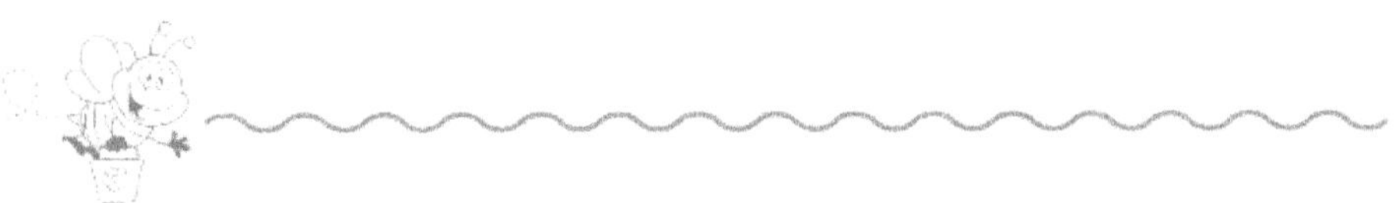

The bee is wearing a pink pacifier to calm itself.

Η μέλισσα φοράει ροζ πιπίλα για να ηρεμήσει.

Name ___________

I Can...

- [ ] read the 1st sentence.
- [ ] read the 2nd sentence.
- [ ] make a sentence from a picture.
- [ ] color a picture.
- [ ] Draw a picture.

The ladybug has many spots.

Η πασχαλίτσα έχει πολλά σημεία.

The red and black ladybug is just done eating some leaves.

Η κόκκινη και μαύρη πασχαλίτσα μόλις τελειώσει τρώει μερικά φύλλα.

Name

I Can...

- [ ] read the 1st sentence.
- [ ] read the 2nd sentence.
- [ ] make a sentence from a picture.
- [ ] color a picture.
- [ ] Draw a picture.

The sheep are skinny.

Τα πρόβατα είναι κοκαλιάρα.

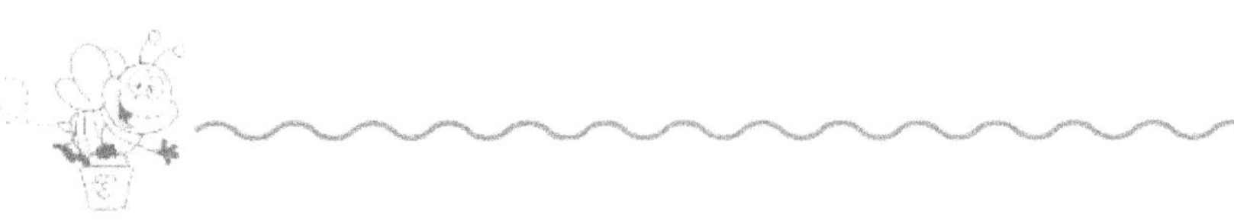

The white sheep have a lot of fluffy white wool to give away.

Το λευκό πρόβατο έχει πολύ αφράτο λευκό μαλλί για να δώσει μακριά.

Name ______________________

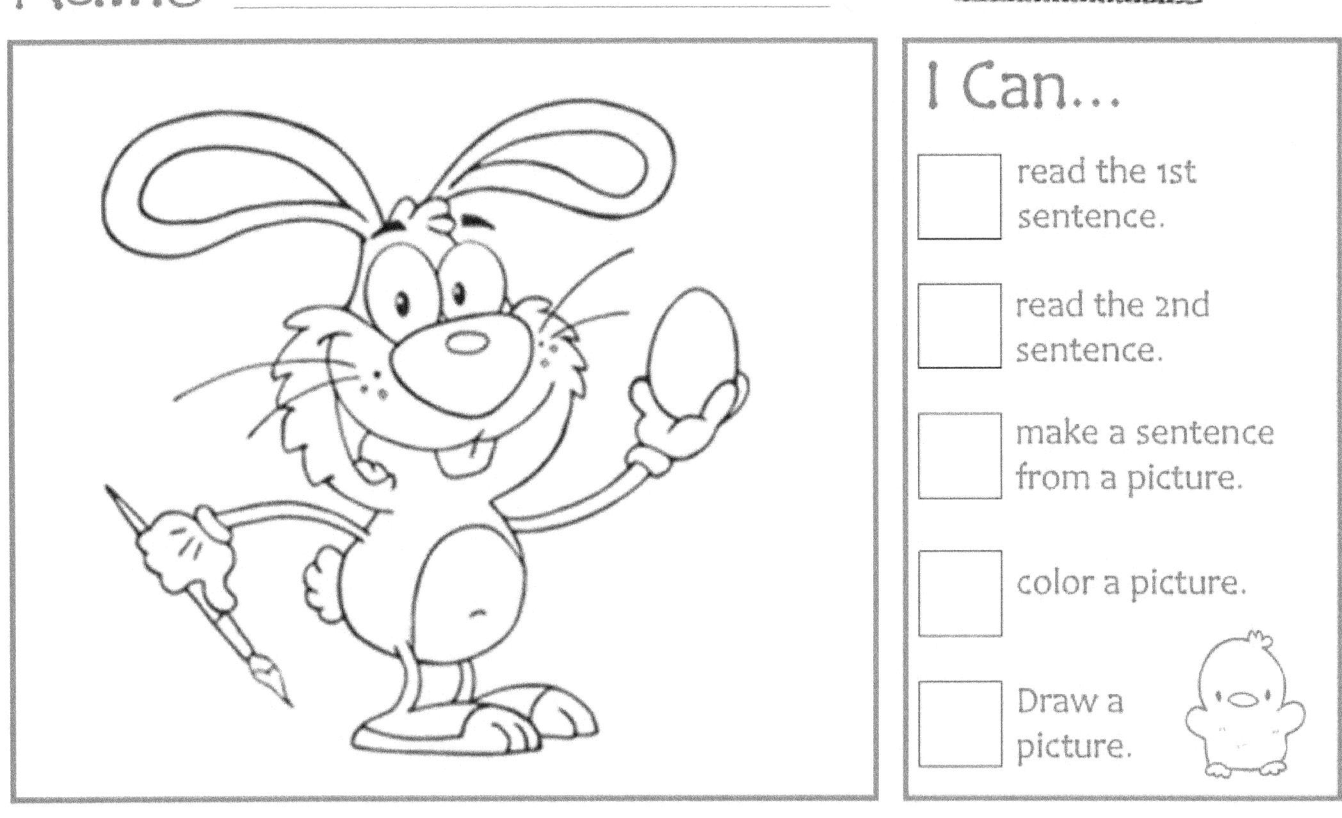

I Can...

- [ ] read the 1st sentence.
- [ ] read the 2nd sentence.
- [ ] make a sentence from a picture.
- [ ] color a picture.
- [ ] Draw a picture.

The rabbit is entering an egg painting contest.

Το κουνέλι μπαίνει σε διαγωνισμό ζωγραφικής αυγών.

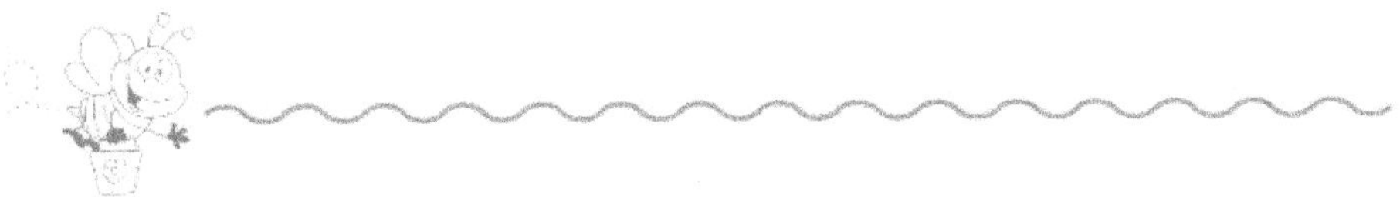

The Easter Bunny is painting a chocolate egg.

Το Πάσχα Μπάνι ζωγραφίζει ένα αυγό σοκολάτας.

Name

I Can...

- [ ] read the 1st sentence.
- [ ] read the 2nd sentence.
- [ ] make a sentence from a picture.
- [ ] color a picture.
- [ ] Draw a picture.

The owl is a language arts teacher.

Η κουκουβάγια είναι καθηγητής γλωσσών.

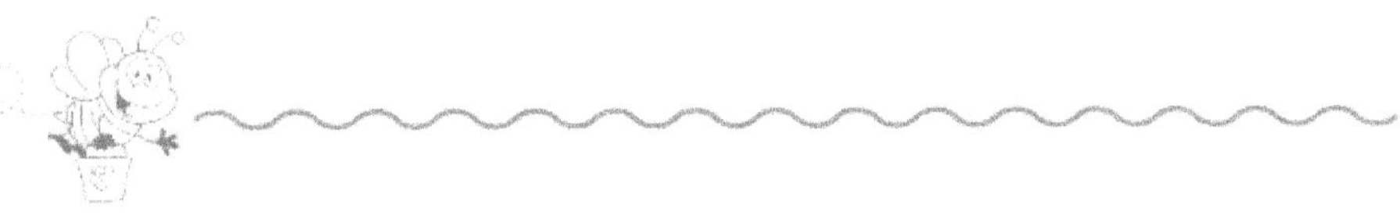

An owl is teaching the kids in school about work.

Μια κουκουβάγια διδάσκει τα παιδιά στο σχολείο για την εργασία.

Name

I Can...

- [ ] read the 1st sentence.
- [ ] read the 2nd sentence.
- [ ] make a sentence from a picture.
- [ ] color a picture.
- [ ] Draw a picture.

The man has an ancient hammer.

Ο άνθρωπος έχει ένα αρχαίο σφυρί.

The builder man has gone to work on a project.

Ο οικοδόμος εργάζεται για ένα έργο.

Name

I Can...

- [ ] read the 1st sentence.
- [ ] read the 2nd sentence.
- [ ] make a sentence from a picture.
- [ ] color a picture.
- [ ] Draw a picture.

The goat has a friend.

Η κατσίκα έχει φίλο.

The old goat is proud of its golden bell.

Η παλιά αίγα είναι υπερήφανη για το χρυσό κουδούνι της.

Name

I Can...

- [ ] read the 1st sentence.
- [ ] read the 2nd sentence.
- [ ] make a sentence from a picture.
- [ ] color a picture.
- [ ] Draw a picture.

My mom's friend is a maid.

Ο φίλος της μαμάς μου είναι κοπέλα.

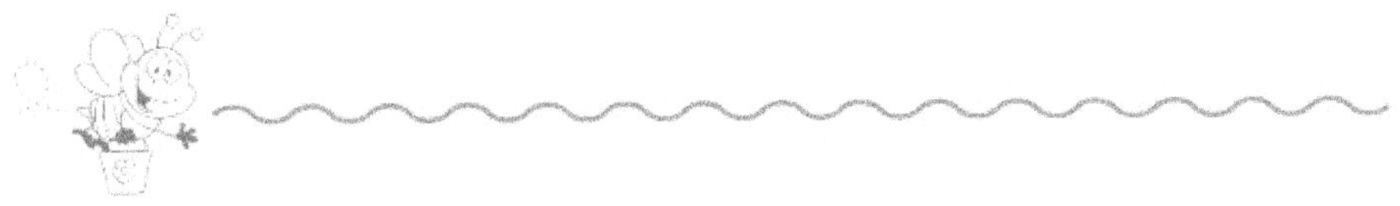

The maid is going to clean the hotel room.

Η καμαριέρα πρόκειται να καθαρίσει το δωμάτιο του ξενοδοχείου.

Name

I Can...

- [ ] read the 1st sentence.
- [ ] read the 2nd sentence.
- [ ] make a sentence from a picture.
- [ ] color a picture.
- [ ] Draw a picture.

I went to the zoo.

Πήγα στο ζωολογικό κήπο.

The animals are having a big celebration.

Τα ζώα έχουν μια μεγάλη γιορτή.

Name _______________________

I Can...

- [ ] read the 1st sentence.
- [ ] read the 2nd sentence.
- [ ] make a sentence from a picture.
- [ ] color a picture.
- [ ] Draw a picture.

The dinosaur has a pillow.

Ο δεινόσαυρος έχει ένα μαξιλάρι.

The dragon is using the rock to build its house.

Ο δράκος χρησιμοποιεί το βράχο για να χτίσει το σπίτι του.

Name

I Can...

- [ ] read the 1st sentence.
- [ ] read the 2nd sentence.
- [ ] make a sentence from a picture.
- [ ] color a picture.
- [ ] Draw a picture.

The boy is excited to go to school.

Το αγόρι είναι ενθουσιασμένο για να πάει στο σχολείο.

The boy is late for school, so he is sprinting.

Το αγόρι καθυστερεί για το σχολείο, οπότε σπριντ.

Name

I Can...

- [ ] read the 1st sentence.
- [ ] read the 2nd sentence.
- [ ] make a sentence from a picture.
- [ ] color a picture.
- [ ] Draw a picture.

The kids on the school bus are going to school.

Τα παιδιά στο σχολικό λεωφορείο πηγαίνουν στο σχολείο.

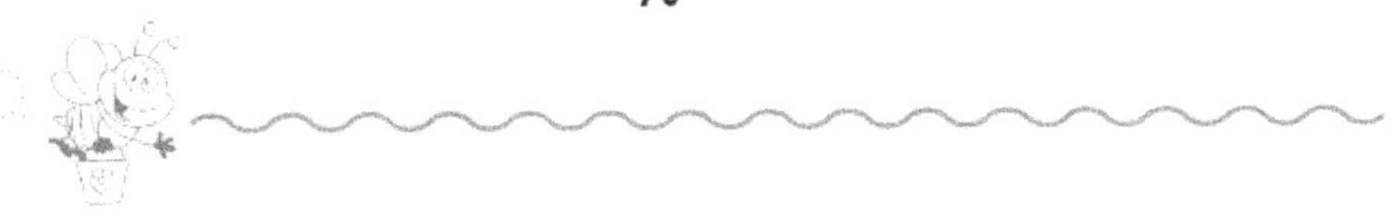

The children are going on a field trip on the yellow bus.

Τα παιδιά πηγαίνουν σε ένα ταξίδι στο κίτρινο λεωφορείο.

Name

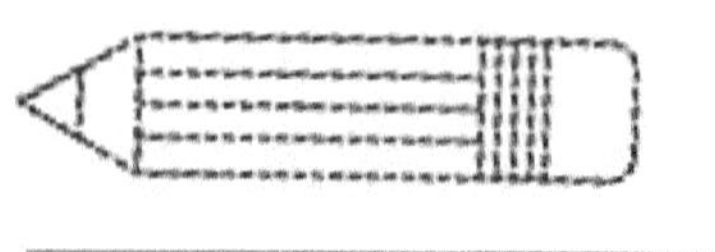

I Can...

- [ ] read the 1st sentence.
- [ ] read the 2nd sentence.
- [ ] make a sentence from a picture.
- [ ] color a picture.
- [ ] Draw a picture.

The cobra is very lovely.

Η κόμπρα είναι πολύ όμορφη.

The rattlesnake is looking for its dinner.

Ο κροταλίας ψάχνει για το δείπνο του.

Name

I Can...

- [ ] read the 1st sentence.
- [ ] read the 2nd sentence.
- [ ] make a sentence from a picture.
- [ ] color a picture.
- [ ] Draw a picture.

That is a fat dog!

Αυτό είναι ένα λιπαρό σκυλί!

This dog is wagging its tail for more treats.

Αυτό το σκυλί κουνάει την ουρά του για περισσότερες απολαύσεις.

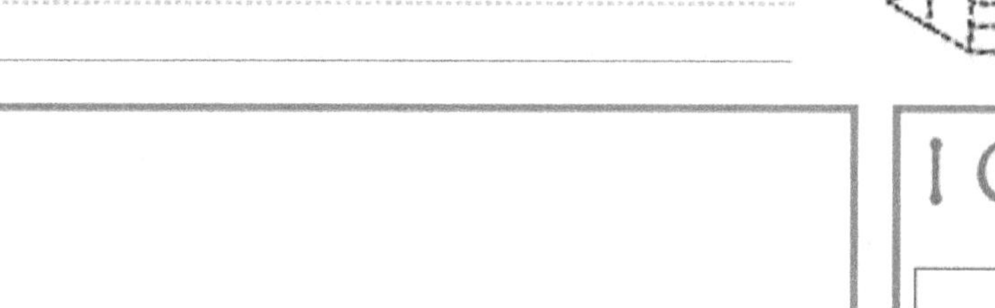

Name

I Can...

- [ ] read the 1st sentence.
- [ ] read the 2nd sentence.
- [ ] make a sentence from a picture.
- [ ] color a picture.
- [ ] Draw a picture.

The elephant lives in the zoo.

Ο ελέφαντας ζει στον ζωολογικό κήπο.

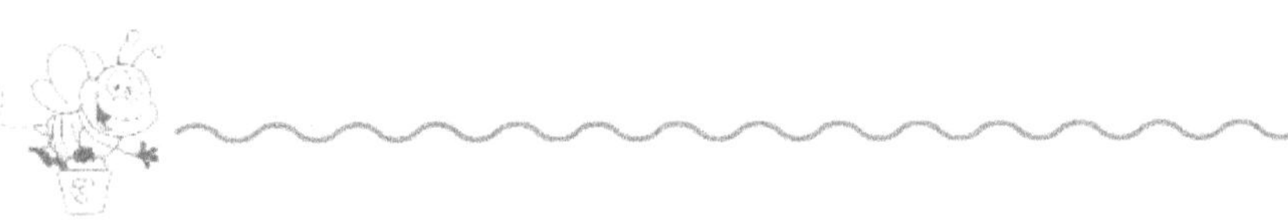

The elephant has a long trunk to spray water.

Ο ελέφαντας έχει ένα μακρύ κορμό για να ψεκάσει το νερό.

Name

I Can...

- [ ] read the 1st sentence.
- [ ] read the 2nd sentence.
- [ ] make a sentence from a picture.
- [ ] color a picture.
- [ ] Draw a picture.

The giraffe eats vegetables.

Η καμηλοπάρδαλη τρώει λαχανικά.

The giraffe has an extremely long neck.

Η καμηλοπάρδαλη έχει εξαιρετικά μεγάλο λαιμό.

Name ___________

I Can...

- [ ] read the 1st sentence.
- [ ] read the 2nd sentence.
- [ ] make a sentence from a picture.
- [ ] color a picture.
- [ ] Draw a picture.

The chipmunk has a soft tummy.

Το chipmunk έχει μια μαλακή κοιλιά.

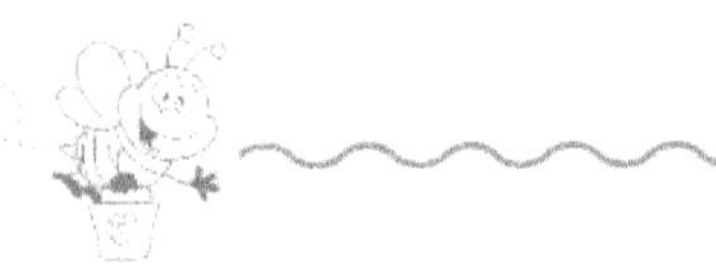

The Chipmunk is about to eat a brown acorn.

Ο Chipmunk πρόκειται να φάει ένα καφέ βελανίδι.

Name

I Can...

- [ ] read the 1st sentence.
- [ ] read the 2nd sentence.
- [ ] make a sentence from a picture.
- [ ] color a picture.
- [ ] Draw a picture.

I have ten toes in total.

Έχω δέκα δάχτυλα συνολικά.

The one and the zero are holding hands.

Το ένα και το μηδέν κρατούν τα χέρια.

Name

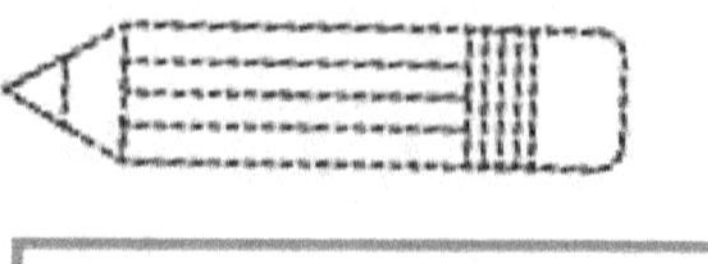

I Can...

- [ ] read the 1st sentence.
- [ ] read the 2nd sentence.
- [ ] make a sentence from a picture.
- [ ] color a picture.
- [ ] Draw a picture.

The alligator is jumping.

Ο αλλιγάτορας είναι άλμα.

The crocodile is excited.

Ο κροκόδειλος είναι ενθουσιασμένος.

Name

I Can...

- [ ] read the 1st sentence.
- [ ] read the 2nd sentence.
- [ ] make a sentence from a picture.
- [ ] color a picture.
- [ ] Draw a picture.

I found an ant.

Βρήκα ένα μυρμήγκι.

The ant is telling a story.

Το μυρμήγκι λέει μια ιστορία.

Name

I Can...

- [ ] read the 1st sentence.
- [ ] read the 2nd sentence.
- [ ] make a sentence from a picture.
- [ ] color a picture.
- [ ] Draw a picture.

The bat sleeps upside down.

Το ρόπαλο κοιμάται ανάποδα.

The bat is ready to fly.

Το ρόπαλο είναι έτοιμο να πετάξει.

Name

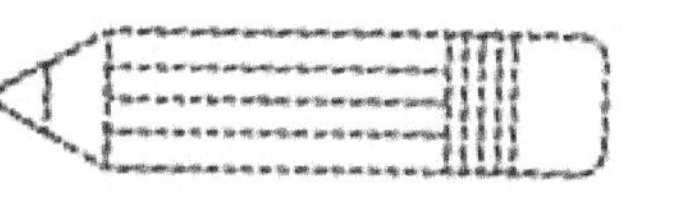

I Can...

- [ ] read the 1st sentence.
- [ ] read the 2nd sentence.
- [ ] make a sentence from a picture.
- [ ] color a picture.
- [ ] Draw a picture.

The cat is very tired.

Η γάτα είναι πολύ κουρασμένη.

The cat is taking a nap.

Η γάτα παίρνει έναν υπνάκο.

Name

I Can...

- [ ] read the 1st sentence.
- [ ] read the 2nd sentence.
- [ ] make a sentence from a picture.
- [ ] color a picture.
- [ ] Draw a picture.

The dog likes to play.

Το σκυλί αρέσει να παίζει.

The dog is playing with a bone.

Το σκυλί παίζει με κόκαλο.

Name

I Can...

- [ ] read the 1st sentence.
- [ ] read the 2nd sentence.
- [ ] make a sentence from a picture.
- [ ] color a picture.
- [ ] Draw a picture.

The elephant has eyelashes.

Ο ελέφαντας έχει βλεφαρίδες.

The elephant is shy.

Ο ελέφαντας είναι ντροπαλός.

Name

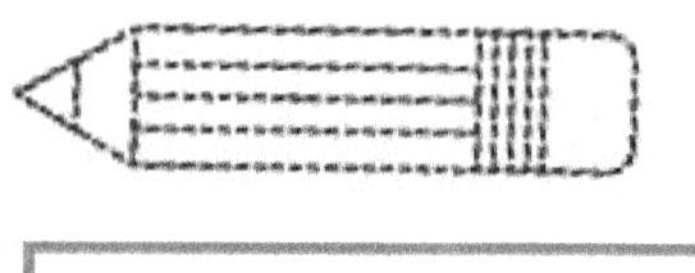

I Can...

- [ ] read the 1st sentence.
- [ ] read the 2nd sentence.
- [ ] make a sentence from a picture.
- [ ] color a picture.
- [ ] Draw a picture.

The frog is hopping.

Ο βάτραχος αναπηδά.

The frog is trying to catch the fly.

Ο βάτραχος προσπαθεί να πιάσει τη μύγα.

Name

I Can...

- [ ] read the 1st sentence.
- [ ] read the 2nd sentence.
- [ ] make a sentence from a picture.
- [ ] color a picture.
- [ ] Draw a picture.

The goat is sleepily walking around.

Η κατσίκα περπατάει ύπνο.

The goat is eating grass.

Η κατσίκα τρώει γρασίδι.

Name

I Can...

- [ ] read the 1st sentence.
- [ ] read the 2nd sentence.
- [ ] make a sentence from a picture.
- [ ] color a picture.
- [ ] Draw a picture.

The hippo has a big head.

Ο ιππότης έχει ένα μεγάλο κεφάλι.

The hippo has a big head.

Ο ιππότης έχει ένα μεγάλο κεφάλι.

Name

I Can...

- [ ] read the 1st sentence.
- [ ] read the 2nd sentence.
- [ ] make a sentence from a picture.
- [ ] color a picture.
- [ ] Draw a picture.

The iguana has a long tail.

Η ιγκουάνα έχει μακρά ουρά.

The iguana is hiding behind the letter I.

Η ιγκουάνα κρύβεται πίσω από το γράμμα I.

Name

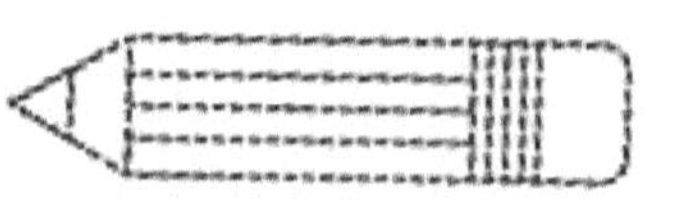

I Can...

- [ ] read the 1st sentence.
- [ ] read the 2nd sentence.
- [ ] make a sentence from a picture.
- [ ] color a picture.
- [ ] Draw a picture.

Mom bought a new bottle of jam.

Το μαμά αγόρασε ένα νέο μπουκάλι μαρμελάδας.

There is jam on the bread.

Υπάρχει μαρμελάδα στο ψωμί.

Name ______________________

I Can...

- [ ] read the 1st sentence.
- [ ] read the 2nd sentence.
- [ ] make a sentence from a picture.
- [ ] color a picture.
- [ ] Draw a picture.

The kite has a beautiful tail.

Ο χαρταετός έχει μια όμορφη ουρά.

The kite is on the ground.

Ο χαρταετός είναι στο έδαφος.

Name

I Can...

- [ ] read the 1st sentence.
- [ ] read the 2nd sentence.
- [ ] make a sentence from a picture.
- [ ] color a picture.
- [ ] Draw a picture.

The lion is timid.

Το λιοντάρι είναι δειλά.

The lion is big.

Το λιοντάρι είναι μεγάλο.

Name

I Can...

- [ ] read the 1st sentence.
- [ ] read the 2nd sentence.
- [ ] make a sentence from a picture.
- [ ] color a picture.
- [ ] Draw a picture.

I like mice.

Μου αρέσουν τα ποντίκια.

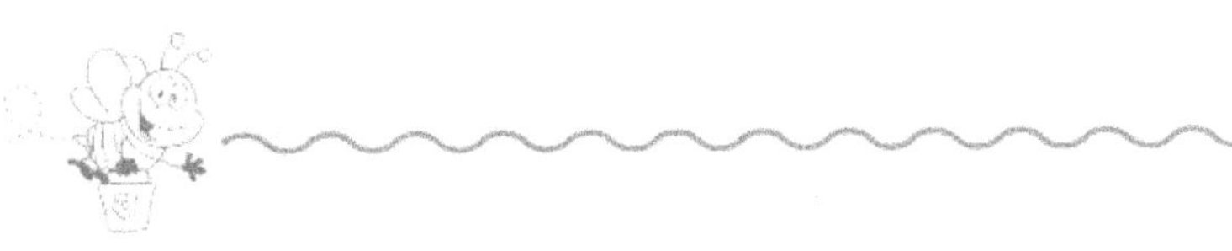

A rat is on top of the letter M

Ένας αρουραίος βρίσκεται πάνω από το γράμμα M

Name 

I Can...

- [ ] read the 1st sentence.
- [ ] read the 2nd sentence.
- [ ] make a sentence from a picture.
- [ ] color a picture.
- [ ] Draw a picture.

The nose is breathing.

Η μύτη αναπνέει.

The letter N stands for a nose.

Το γράμμα N σημαίνει μύτη.

Name

I Can...

- [ ] read the 1st sentence.
- [ ] read the 2nd sentence.
- [ ] make a sentence from a picture.
- [ ] color a picture.
- [ ] Draw a picture.

The octopus lives underwater.

Το χταπόδι ζει υποβρύχια.

The octopus has eight tentacles.

Το χταπόδι έχει οκτώ πλοκάμια.

Name

I Can...

- [ ] read the 1st sentence.
- [ ] read the 2nd sentence.
- [ ] make a sentence from a picture.
- [ ] color a picture.
- [ ] Draw a picture.

The penguin eats fish.

Ο πιγκουίνος τρώει ψάρι.

The penguin lives in the arctic.

Ο πιγκουίνος ζει στην αρκτική.

Name ________________

I Can...

- ☐ read the 1st sentence.
- ☐ read the 2nd sentence.
- ☐ make a sentence from a picture.
- ☐ color a picture.
- ☐ Draw a picture.

The queen has a wand.

Η βασίλισσα έχει μια ραβδί.

The queen is beautiful.

Η βασίλισσα είναι όμορφη.

Name

I Can...

- [ ] read the 1st sentence.
- [ ] read the 2nd sentence.
- [ ] make a sentence from a picture.
- [ ] color a picture.
- [ ] Draw a picture.

The rabbit has long ears.

Το κουνέλι έχει μακρά αυτιά.

The rabbit is thinking about something.

Το κουνέλι σκέφτεται κάτι.

Name

I Can...

- [ ] read the 1st sentence.
- [ ] read the 2nd sentence.
- [ ] make a sentence from a picture.
- [ ] color a picture.
- [ ] Draw a picture.

The snake has polka dots.

Το φίδι έχει πολικές τελείες.

The snake is licking its lip because it is hungry.

Το φίδι γλείφει το χείλι του επειδή είναι πεινασμένο.

Name ______________

I Can...

- [ ] read the 1st sentence.
- [ ] read the 2nd sentence.
- [ ] make a sentence from a picture.
- [ ] color a picture.
- [ ] Draw a picture.

The tortoise has a pointy shell.

Η χελώνα έχει ένα μυτερό κέλυφος.

The turtle has a robust shell but is very slow.

Η χελώνα έχει ένα γερό κέλυφος, αλλά είναι πολύ αργή.

Name

I Can...

- [ ] read the 1st sentence.
- [ ] read the 2nd sentence.
- [ ] make a sentence from a picture.
- [ ] color a picture.
- [ ] Draw a picture.

It's raining.

Βρέχει.

We use the umbrella when it's raining.

Χρησιμοποιούμε την ομπρέλα όταν βρέχει.

I Can...

- [ ] read the 1st sentence.
- [ ] read the 2nd sentence.
- [ ] make a sentence from a picture.
- [ ] color a picture.
- [ ] Draw a picture.

The violin is a musical instrument.

Το βιολί είναι ένα μουσικό όργανο.

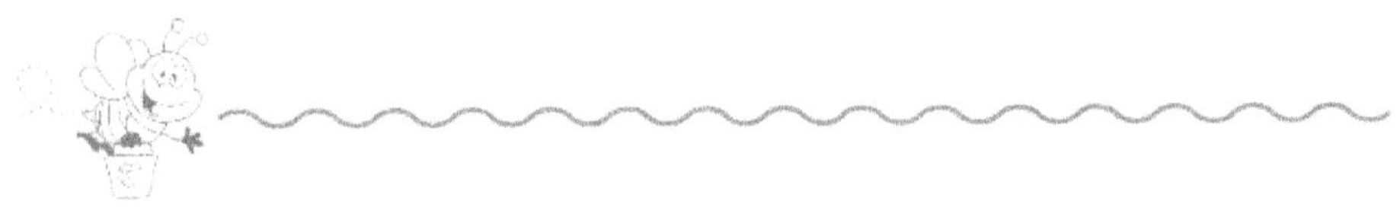

A violin can play beautiful music if played correctly.

Ένα βιολί μπορεί να παίξει όμορφη μουσική εάν παίζεται σωστά.

106

I Can...

- [ ] read the 1st sentence.
- [ ] read the 2nd sentence.
- [ ] make a sentence from a picture.
- [ ] color a picture.
- [ ] Draw a picture.

The walrus has a friend.

Ο θάλαμος έχει φίλο.

____

The walrus has unusually sharp teeth.

Ο ορτύκι έχει ασυνήθιστα αιχμηρά δόντια.

Name

I Can...

- [ ] read the 1st sentence.
- [ ] read the 2nd sentence.
- [ ] make a sentence from a picture.
- [ ] color a picture.
- [ ] Draw a picture.

The xylophone is a colorful instrument.

Το ξυλόφωνο είναι ένα πολύχρωμο όργανο.

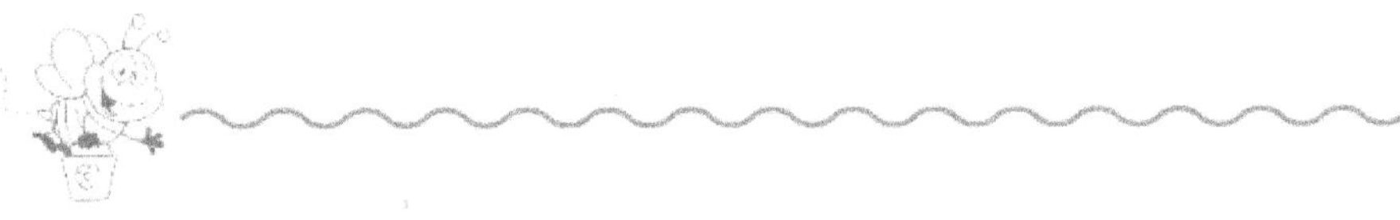

The xylophone is an instrument like the piano.

Το ξυλόφωνο είναι ένα όργανο σαν το πιάνο.

Name

I Can...

- [ ] read the 1st sentence.
- [ ] read the 2nd sentence.
- [ ] make a sentence from a picture.
- [ ] color a picture.
- [ ] Draw a picture.

The boy has a little hat.

Το αγόρι έχει ένα μικρό καπέλο.

The boy is having fun playing with a yoyo.

Το αγόρι διασκεδάζει με ένα yoyo.

I Can...

- [ ] read the 1st sentence.
- [ ] read the 2nd sentence.
- [ ] make a sentence from a picture.
- [ ] color a picture.
- [ ] Draw a picture.

The zebra has a tail.

Η ζέβρα έχει μια ουρά.

The zebra has black and white stripes.

Η ζέβρα έχει ασπρόμαυρες λωρίδες.

Name

I Can...

- [ ] read the 1st sentence.
- [ ] read the 2nd sentence.
- [ ] make a sentence from a picture.
- [ ] color a picture.
- [ ] Draw a picture.

I have a candle on my cake.

Έχω ένα κερί στο κέικ μου.

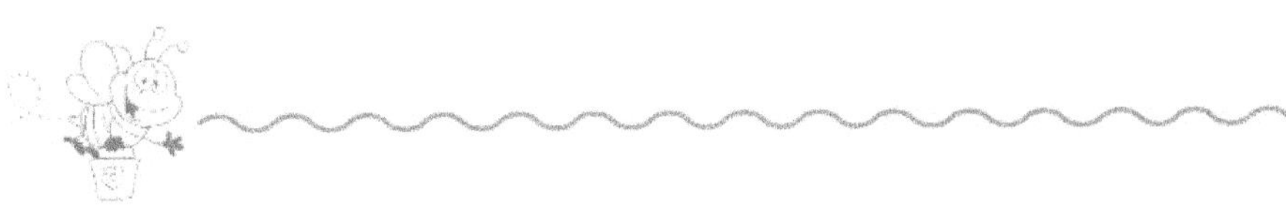

I had a small birthday cake for my party.

Είχα μια μικρή τούρτα γενεθλίων για το κόμμα μου.

I Can...

- [ ] read the 1st sentence.
- [ ] read the 2nd sentence.
- [ ] make a sentence from a picture.
- [ ] color a picture.
- [ ] Draw a picture.

The astronaut is going on a mission.

Ο αστροναύτης πηγαίνει σε μια αποστολή.

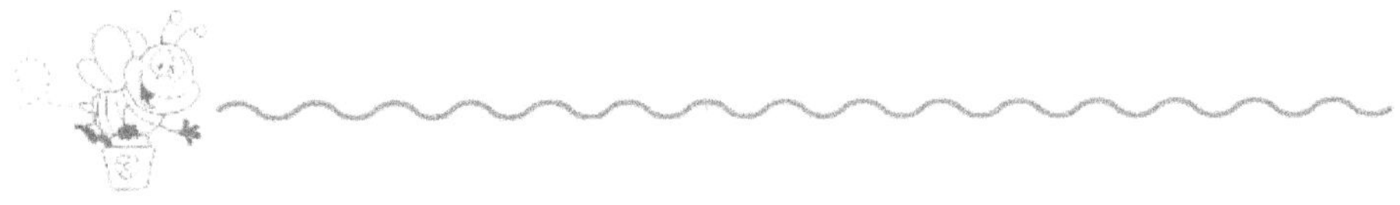

An astronaut has to explore our universe so that we would have more knowledge.

Ένας αστροναύτης πρέπει να εξερευνήσει το σύμπαν μας για να έχουμε περισσότερες γνώσεις.

I Can...

- [ ] read the 1st sentence.
- [ ] read the 2nd sentence.
- [ ] make a sentence from a picture.
- [ ] color a picture.
- [ ] Draw a picture.

The samurai is going for a morning jog.

Ο σαμουράι πηγαίνει για πρωινή jog.

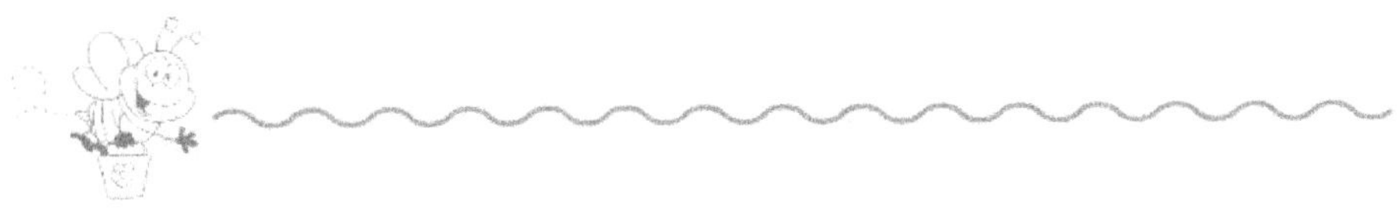

The samurai is training to become good at fighting.

Ο σαμουράι είναι κατάρτιση για να γίνει καλός στην πάλη.

Name ___________________

I Can...

- [ ] read the 1st sentence.
- [ ] read the 2nd sentence.
- [ ] make a sentence from a picture.
- [ ] color a picture.
- [ ] Draw a picture.

My friend is having a gigantic cake.

Ο φίλος μου έχει μια γιγαντιαία τούρτα.

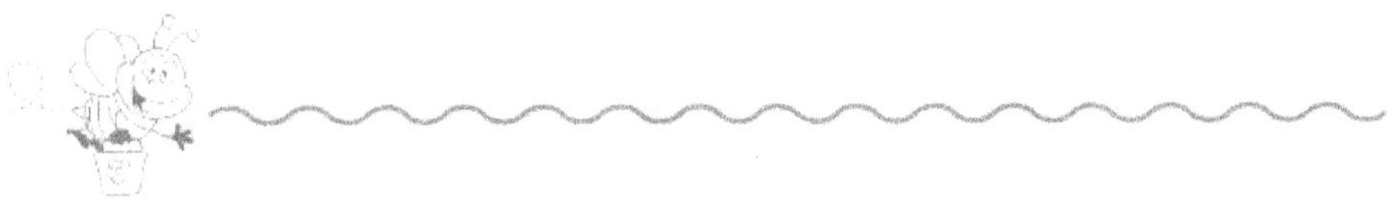

I had a humongous birthday cake for my celebration.

Είχα μια τεράστια τούρτα γενεθλίων για τον εορτασμό μου.

Name

I Can...

- [ ] read the 1st sentence.
- [ ] read the 2nd sentence.
- [ ] make a sentence from a picture.
- [ ] color a picture.
- [ ] Draw a picture.

The frog is chasing the fly.

Ο βάτραχος κυνηγάει τη μύγα.

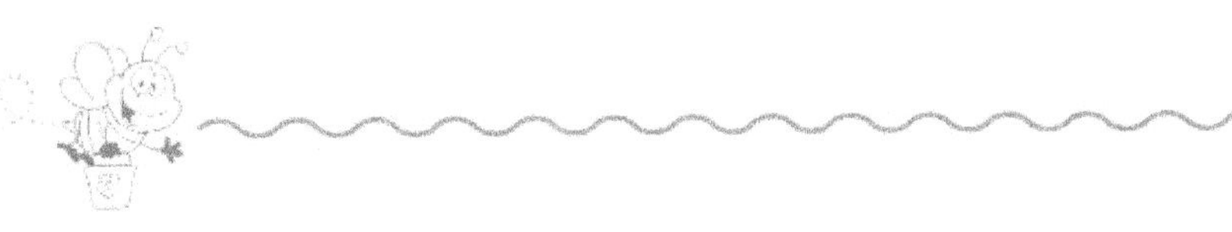

The green frog is trying to catch the fly.

Ο πράσινος βάτραχος προσπαθεί να πιάσει τη μύγα.

Name ____________________

I Can...

- [ ] read the 1st sentence.
- [ ] read the 2nd sentence.
- [ ] make a sentence from a picture.
- [ ] color a picture.
- [ ] Draw a picture.

The ladybug has six legs.

Η πασχαλίτσα έχει έξι πόδια.

The ladybug is on the leaf.

Η πασχαλίτσα βρίσκεται στο φύλλο.

Name

I Can...

- [ ] read the 1st sentence.
- [ ] read the 2nd sentence.
- [ ] make a sentence from a picture.
- [ ] color a picture.
- [ ] Draw a picture.

The dragon is sick.

Ο δράκος είναι άρρωστος.

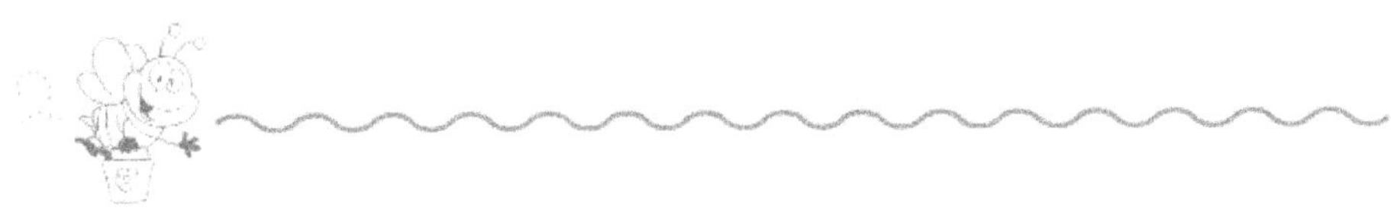

The dragon just ate something spicy, so he needed water.

Ο δράκος έφαγε μόνο κάτι πικάντικο, οπότε χρειαζόταν νερό.

Name

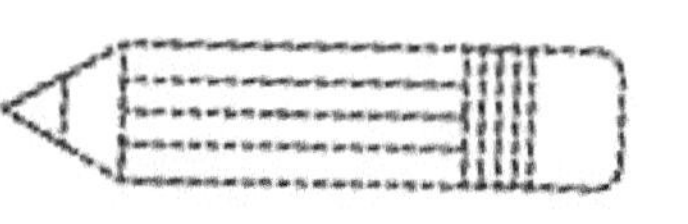

I Can...

- [ ] read the 1st sentence.
- [ ] read the 2nd sentence.
- [ ] make a sentence from a picture.
- [ ] color a picture.
- [ ] Draw a picture.

That is a baby cow.

Αυτή είναι μια αγελάδα.

A little cow is walking around near the barn.

Μια μικρή αγελάδα περπατάει κοντά στον αχυρώνα.

Name

I Can...

- [ ] read the 1st sentence.
- [ ] read the 2nd sentence.
- [ ] make a sentence from a picture.
- [ ] color a picture.
- [ ] Draw a picture.

The frog has a big smile.

Ο βάτραχος έχει ένα μεγάλο χαμόγελο.

The frog is smiling because it is happy.

Ο βάτραχος χαμογελάει επειδή είναι χαρούμενος.

Name

I Can...

- [ ] read the 1st sentence.
- [ ] read the 2nd sentence.
- [ ] make a sentence from a picture.
- [ ] color a picture.
- [ ] Draw a picture.

The frog has a big mouth.

Ο βάτραχος έχει ένα μεγάλο στόμα.

The frog is waving to us.

Ο βάτραχος κυλά σε μας.